Count Me In
Jewish Wisdom in Action

TEACHING GUIDE

Vicki Lieberman

www.behrmanhouse.com

Project Manager: Gila Gevirtz
Designer: Stacey May

Copyright © 2005 by Behrman House, Inc.
Springfield, New Jersey
www.behrmanhouse.com

ISBN 0-87441-195-5
Manufactured in the United States of America

Contents

Introduction

Introduction to the Textbook

Count Me In: Jewish Wisdom in Action invites students to explore Jewish values. It does so by focusing on the everyday relationships and decisions that are integral to their lives; for example, when to help a friend and when to care for themselves, what to do when they feel jealous of a sibling or classmate, and how to make sound judgments in difficult situations. It teaches students to use the wisdom of Jewish sacred texts—Torah, Prophets, Writings, and Talmud—as the lens through which to view these concerns.

Through a rich array of stories, source material, critical-thinking activities, and opportunities for students to apply what they have learned, the textbook not only invites students to explore the ethical underpinnings of Judaism, but also to explore the relationship between knowledge and action. Students learn that the purpose of Jewish study—*talmud Torah*—is to guide our behavior so that each of us can contribute to the fulfillment of our people's Covenant with God. In the process, students are encouraged to reflect on their personal values, their goals, and their relationships with others.

Structure of the Textbook

The first chapter—"Wisdom and Action"—introduces the premise that the purpose of Jewish study is to provide guidance for our actions. Each chapter of *Count Me In* that follows presents a specific value, among them free will, community, and peace. Every chapter opens with a quote from *Pirkei Avot* and closes with a quote from Psalm 119. To enrich the authenticity of the learning experience, Hebrew (along with English translation) appears in several of the chapter features. You may have the students read the Hebrew or simply acknowledge that the text was originally written in Hebrew.

Throughout each chapter there are a variety of sidebars with interesting enrichments and opportunities for student interaction and reflection. For example, in the chapter "The Value of Free Will," students are given the opportunity to reflect on what life might be like if humans didn't have free will and to discuss what helps

1

them make good choices (treat others with respect) when they are tempted to make poor ones (gossip). In addition, each chapter that explores a specific value includes the following special features:

✳ Opening Story Each chapter's value is introduced through a story. These stories come from a variety of sources, including biblical and Talmudic texts, Jewish folklore, and modern literature.

✳ Bible Bio A biblical character is portrayed in light of the chapter value. For example, the chapter "The Value of Argument" presents the story of Abraham arguing with God about the destruction of Sodom and Gomorrah.

✳ The Extraordinary Acts of Ordinary People Here the spotlight is on modern Jews who exemplify the tradition of living Jewish values. Examples are philanthropist Jacob Henry Schiff, political and social activist Bella Abzug, and workers' rights organizer Clara Lemlich.

✳ Ancient Stories for Modern Times Drawn from a variety of traditional Jewish sources, these stories are followed by questions that help students apply the values they teach to their own lives.

✳ Learn It & Live It These closing activities help students reflect on and integrate what they have learned and help them take actions based on their new knowledge.

Structure of the Teaching Guide

This teaching guide is designed to help you use *Count Me In* easily and effectively. It includes a variety of activities that engage a full range of learning modalities: probing questions that stimulate critical thinking and class discussion, step-by-step directions for art projects, collaborative learning environments, and creative activities for family participation. Where appropriate, the guide also provides answers to questions in the textbook.

Most importantly, the suggestions in the guide can be easily adapted to your personal teaching style, and to the strengths and interests of your students. To help you succeed, before selecting an activity, consider the many factors that come into play in your class, such as time constraints and students' abilities and maturity level.

Each chapter in the teaching guide beyond the introductory chapter complements a chapter in the textbook and includes the following elements:

✳ Core Concept A brief summary of the chapter's central, governing idea

✳ Learning Objectives Goals for students to achieve by the end of the chapter

✳ Chapter Overview A brief statement about the chapter content

✳ Key Vocabulary Definitions of key words that appear in the chapter

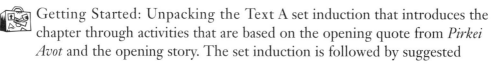 Getting Started: Unpacking the Text A set induction that introduces the chapter through activities that are based on the opening quote from *Pirkei Avot* and the opening story. The set induction is followed by suggested

teaching techniques for the chapter, including small group and class discussions, artwork, creative writing, and role playing.

 Artist's Corner A theme-related art activity. In most cases, the only art supplies you will need are those commonly found in schools. Feel free to customize the materials to suit your class. These activities can be used to create classroom or school displays.

 Teaching Enrichment An opportunity for students to engage in a thought-provoking conversation that challenges a concept or value that is presented in the chapter.

 Photo Op A discussion that uses a photograph or artwork in the textbook as a jumping-off point.

 Family in Action Suggestions for how students and their families can plan actions they can take based on the Jewish value explored in the chapter.

Many of the questions posed in the textbook and teaching guide are open-ended and personal in nature, and lend themselves to a multitude of appropriate responses. Use these questions—such as those posed in the "Learn It & Live It" and "Teaching Enrichment" activities—to encourage open discussion and the sharing of personal opinions, ideas, and experiences.

Finally, remember that it is the relationship your students have with you and their classmates that will largely determine the success of the learning process. Create a positive environment by developing a comfort level with the book's contents, welcoming the ideas of all your students, and creating an atmosphere of acceptance and tolerance. Most importantly, model the Jewish values you are teaching.

Wishing you and your students every success.

Introducing Count Me In to Students

Introduce your class to *Count Me In* by building on students' existing knowledge. Begin by distributing the book and asking students what the title, subtitle, and cover images suggest the book will be about. *(Jewish values, Israel, peace, Torah)* Ask: What does the expression "count me in" mean? *(I want to participate.)* What might the book be about participating in?" *(Jewish life, Jewish values, Jewish activities)*

Invite students to read the table of contents. Brainstorm a definition of "value." *(priority, something worthwhile, a good way to behave)* Ask: What makes a value a Jewish value? *(It's taught in the Torah. Jewish people think it's important. Rabbis teach it.)*

Give the class a few minutes to skim *Count Me In* and to offer additional thoughts on what the book is about. Then have them turn to page 5 (immediately following the table of contents). Invite several volunteers to each read a paragraph. Ask: Do you think that studying the wisdom of sages from centuries ago can help us live better lives today? *(Yes: because their wisdom has been tested by time. No: because we live in a very different world.)* Tell students that as they read *Count Me In*, they will have many opportunities to consider when and how they might benefit from the lessons our sages taught.

CHAPTER 1

Wisdom AND Action

Textbook pages 6–17

Core Concept

The purpose of Jewish learning is to acquire the necessary wisdom to guide our actions. Through study we learn to take the actions that help us become our best selves and contribute to making the world a better place.

Learning Objectives

Students will be able to:

◎ Describe several ways in which they can honor the Jewish people's Covenant, or *Brit*, with God.

◎ Differentiate between the Written Law (Bible) and Oral Law (Talmud).

◎ Draw from personal examples and from the lives of others to explain how studying Jewish values can lead to a fairer and more just world.

Chapter Overview

This chapter teaches that the purpose of gaining Jewish wisdom (studying Torah and other sacred teachings) is to help us learn to take sacred actions, such as feeding the hungry, comforting the ill, and respecting our elders. Students learn that the Jewish people entered into a covenant with God and were given the Torah, which provides us with the instructions for living as a holy people.

Key Vocabulary

Am Kadosh Holy nation

Brit Covenant; the agreement between God and the Jewish people

Mitzvah, Mitzvot Sacred commandment(s), instruction(s)

 ## Getting Started: Unpacking the Text

(pages 6–7)

Invite a student to read *Pirkei Avot* 3:17 on page 6. Ask students to what kind of "deeds" they think Rabbi Elazar was referring. (*good deeds*, mitzvot, *acts of kindness and caring*) Ask students how they would describe a person whose wisdom is greater than his or her deeds. (*person knows a lot but does little or nothing with that knowledge*)

Ask what Rabbi Elazar meant when he compared people with much wisdom but few deeds to trees with many branches but few roots. (*As roots strengthen a tree with many branches so that it can stand upright, so a person with wisdom is strengthened and made more upright by the good actions he or she performs.*) Provide several examples of how taking action can strengthen a person who has much knowledge but little practical experience. (*Playing a musical instrument or reading Hebrew can turn general or abstract knowledge into practical skills, broaden the person's experience and knowledge, and enable the person to help others.*)

Explain that Rabbi Elazar was particularly referring to the wisdom of Torah and the deeds of *mitzvot*, the sacred commandments of Torah. Provide students with several examples of *mitzvot* and ask them to name others. (*studying Torah, giving tzedakah, lighting Shabbat candles*) You may want to make a list on the chalkboard.

Invite a student to the front of the room to read the story on page 7. Then ask: Who in the story says that wisdom (study of Torah) is most important? (*Rabbi Akiva*) Who says that deeds (performing *mitzvot*) are most important? (*Rabbi Tarfon*) Divide the class into two debate teams, one representing Rabbi Akiva's view and the other Rabbi Tarfon's. Hold a five-minute debate and then explain to the students that they will learn about the value of wisdom and action in this chapter.

Our Sacred Covenant *(page 8)*

Divide students into small groups. Distribute a sheet of paper and a pencil to each group. Ask students to list ten members of the Covenant from Jewish history. *(Possible answers: Abraham, Sarah, King David, Maimonides, Theodor Herzl, Golda Meir)* To help students you may want to make copies of the Bible or Ḥumash (Five Books of Moses) available from your sanctuary, as well as Jewish history books. Have students share their lists with the class. Then invite students to add their own names to their lists.

Next to their names, ask students to list three ways in which they honor the *Brit*. *(Possible answers: attend religious school and prayer services, feed a family pet, honor their parents)*

Artist's Corner: Our Sacred Covenant *(page 8)*

After completing the activity above, you may want to make a composite list that includes the names of the famous people from each group and the names of all your students. The list can be written on butcher-block paper or on a large sheet of construction paper. Students can use crayons, highlighters, markers, and colored pencils to decorate the list with pictures of themselves and others honoring the *Brit* through *mitzvot*. You may want to display the results under the title "We Are Members of the *Brit* and Part of Jewish History."

Teaching Enrichment: Our Sacred Teachings *(pages 8–13)*

Before beginning this section, you may want to explain that there are two types of *mitzvot*: ritual *mitzvot* (holiday and religious observances and traditions such as conducting a Passover seder, lighting Ḥanukkah candles, attending prayer services) and ethical *mitzvot* (how we treat others and the world around us; for example, feeding the hungry, being honest, conserving energy). The prophets Isaiah and Hosea taught (see textbook top of page 12) that fulfilling ritual *mitzvot* has value only if we also observe ethical *mitzvot*. Have students debate or discuss whether or not they agree or disagree with the prophets. You may want to invite your rabbi or educational director to join in the debate.

What Are Your Dreams? *(page 9)*

To help students answer the last question, suggest they look at the textbook's table of contents to find values that will help them achieve their dreams. Ask students to share their examples of how what they learn in religious school can help them succeed. *(Possible answers: getting good grades requires persistence and study; getting along with others may require acts of peacemaking)*

Ancient Stories for Modern Times *(page 11)*

Possible answers: attend religious school, help a younger sibling with homework, donate tzedakah

 **Photo Op** (page 12, bottom)

Does fishing or hunting for sport reflect Jewish values? (*Because there is no direct prohibition, we must look to other Jewish values to inform us. The Jewish obligation to be compassionate to animals* [tza'ar ba'alei ḥayyim] *suggests that fishing and hunting for sport are not acceptable.*) A note regarding the killing of animals for food: Judaism strives not to make unnecessary and impractical demands. It recognizes that human beings have a desire to eat meat. Even so, Judaism maintains that animals being raised or hunted for food be treated with compassion.

The Written Law and the Oral Law (page 13)

Have three students each read aloud a paragraph to the class. Then divide the class into two groups. Ask one group to list the advantages of passing down the Oral Law by word of mouth. (*It insures that people will study with others; encourages Jews to live near one another; students must pay close attention to their teachers.*) Have the second group list the advantages of permanently writing down the Oral Law. (*Lessons will not be lost; books can reach a wider audience; people can study whenever they have time.*) Ask: Do you think the benefits of recording the Oral Law outweigh the benefits of passing it on by word of mouth?

 **Photo Op** (page 14)

Ask students to describe a Jewish tradition their families value and to explain why. (*Possible answers: celebrating Passover together because it makes them feel closer, lighting Shabbat candles makes them feel calm, planting trees on Tu B'Shevat helps the environment*)

Learn It & Live It (page 14)

This chapter introduces many examples—honoring parents, recycling, holiday observance—of putting the wisdom of our sacred texts into actions. Invite students to respond to this section's opening question, "How do you know how well you've succeeded in your study of Jewish sacred texts and values?" (*can explain a Jewish text, can read Hebrew, can chant more prayers each year, donate tzedakah each week, treat others with respect*)

 Family in Action

You may want to send a letter home to parents to introduce them to the family activities to which they will be invited to participate in the upcoming chapters. A sample letter is shown on page 7.

Sample Letter to Parents or Guardians

Shalom,

This year, our class will study Jewish values using the textbook *Count Me In: Jewish Wisdom in Action*. Among the values we will explore are persistence, study, community, and peace. In the course of our studies, we will focus on the everyday relationships and decisions that are critical to your child, your family, and our community. We will then investigate how the wisdom found in Jewish sacred texts, such as the Bible and Talmud, can enrich these relationships and guide our decisions and actions.

To reinforce what your child has learned and to encourage your child to act based on this new knowledge, you will periodically be invited to participate in an activity. Your participation will help affirm the importance of your child's religious school studies by tying your family's values into the Jewish values we are studying.

We hope you find the activities engaging and enjoyable, and that they stimulate meaningful family dialogue and enrich your child's appreciation of Jewish tradition.

Thank you for your interest.

Sincerely,

CHAPTER 2

THE Value OF Life

Textbook pages 18–27

Core Concept
Judaism teaches us to value and respect others and ourselves because every person is created in God's image.

Learning Objectives
Students will be able to:

✷ Explain why all human life has equal value.

✷ Articulate what being created in God's image means by providing examples of godly actions human beings can take.

✷ Differentiate between self-esteem and selfishness.

✷ Take actions that show respect for themselves and for others.

Chapter Overview
This chapter teaches the Torah concept that all humans—Jew and non-Jew alike—are created in the image of God. To be made in God's image is to have the capacity to behave in godly ways; for example, by performing acts of kindness and being compassionate and loyal.

Key Vocabulary
B'tzelem Elohim Created in God's image

 Getting Started: Unpacking the Text

(pages 18–19)

Ask students how they might feel if they learned that someone wanted to be their friend but had never told them so. Have students explain their responses. *(Possible answers: disappointed because I might have been friendlier toward the person, glad because I would have felt embarrassed, sad because I might have gotten to know the person better)*

Invite a student to read *Pirkei Avot* 3:14 on page 18. Explain that in this chapter, they will learn about what it means to be created in God's image. Invite students to guess what this means and how knowing it might make them feel special. *(Possible answers: Something about us is like God and knowing it makes me proud; we have a close relationship with God and knowing it makes me feel responsible.)* Welcome all speculation; do not judge any answers. After reading the section "In the Image of God" on pages 20 and 22, you may want to return to this quote and discuss it again with your students.

Have students read the story on page 19. Ask why having the two notes might be helpful. *(reminds them to keep a balanced view; cheers them when they are sad and brings them back to reality when they are getting a bit full of themselves)* Present the students with several situations and ask them which of the two notes they would reach for in those situations and why. Sample situations might include: trying out for a sports team, going to class the first day in a new school, and writing an acceptance speech after winning a school election. Encourage respectful discussion and note that different students may make different choices.

Explain to the students that in this chapter they will learn about the value of all human life—their lives and the lives of others.

 **Artist's Corner: Pirkei Avot 3:14** *(page 18)*

Distribute a sheet of drawing or construction paper and colored pencils or crayons to each student. Ask students to fold the paper in half so that they have two square, or close to square, shapes. Explore the concept of "a special love" by having students draw a heart on the left side of the paper. Inside the heart, ask students to list the people with whom they share a special love. *(parents, friends, siblings)* Outside the heart, have students list ways that special love is made known to them. *(The person gives hugs and kisses; the person is especially giving or helpful.)* God's special love for humanity is made known through the Torah's teaching that we are created in God's image, a very special honor.

　　Now invite students to draw a Torah scroll on the right side of the page. Inside the scroll have them write "I was made in the image of God." Tell students that in this chapter, they will learn about the actions they can take to make it known that they were made in God's image. Have students write their names on their papers, collect the papers, and redistribute them when you complete the chapter. At that point, invite students to list around the scroll the actions they can take. *(Examples: speak honestly and respectfully, help those in need, show compassion to others.)* You may want to display the papers on a bulletin board under the heading "In God's Image."

In the Image of God *(pages 20 and 22)*

Ask students: How can all of us be made in God's image? *(Being made in God's image means we have the ability to behave in godly ways. Just as God clothed Adam and Eve, we can clothe others. Just as God visited Abraham when he was recovering [from his circumcision], we can comfort people who are ill.)* We act in godly ways when we use our abilities to add goodness to the world.

Photo Op *(page 22)*

Ask students to describe how Lydie Egosi's body and soul might have worked together to create her tapestry of Noah's ark. *(Her soul inspired her to turn the Bible story into a beautiful piece of art; her brain, eyes, and hands helped her make the art.)* Ask students for examples of when their own bodies and souls work together. *(Possible answers: praying, visiting someone who is ill, collecting food for the local pantry)* How does this make them feel? *(accomplished, proud, happy)*

Value Yourself *(page 22)*

After reading the story of Hillel, invite student volunteers one at a time to stand on one leg and teach everything they know about Torah to the class; for example, Bible stories and *mitzvot* they know. Presumably your students will not be able to remain on one leg while teaching all they know, and even those who do stay standing won't know all of the Torah.

　　After each student who wants a chance has had one, ask students if they think the man in the story acted respectfully toward Hillel. *(No: The man was rude because*

he challenged Hillel to do the impossible.) In answering the man's question as he did, Hillel followed his own teaching—"What is hateful to you do not do to any person"—demonstrating self-respect and respect for the man.

 ## Teaching Enrichment: Value Yourself *(pages 22–24)*

Conduct a thought-provoking conversation that challenges the Torah commandment to "love your neighbor as yourself." Say: It's easy to love people who are nice, but what about people who are not kind or trustworthy? Ask students for examples of types of people whom they would have difficulty loving. *(school bullies, terrorists, thieves)* Ask whether it's realistic with regard to such people to follow the Torah's commandment to love your neighbor.

Point out that loving your neighbors can also mean keeping them safe from harming themselves or others. We can imprison criminals and provide medical attention for the criminally insane. You may want to invite the rabbi to participate in this discussion.

Value Yourself *(pages 22–24)*

Ask students to read the paragraphs about self-esteem on pages 23 and 24. Encourage them to consider how they might respond to the scenario of the friend who needed help in Spanish, described on page 24. Select three volunteers to participate in a role-playing activity. One student will be the friend needing help, another the one being asked for help, and the third will role-play the parent of the friend being asked for help. Solicit questions from the class for the actors to answer. *(Possible questions: Will you help your friend? How will you persuade your friend to help? Can the parent change the bedtime? Can the parent offer suggestions such as meeting the friend early before school?)*

Bible Bio *(page 23)* and Extraordinary Acts *(page 24)*

Invite students to find similarities between the actions of Bityah and Henrietta Szold. *(Both helped others; both valued the lives of others; both were compassionate.)* Did they solve all their community's problems? *(No. Bityah could not save all the Israelite boys, but she did save one, Moses, who in turn saved the entire people of Israel. Henrietta Szold could not save all the people in Palestine, but she did save thousands.)*

Help students understand through the example of these women that although none of us can completely solve a major problem such as world poverty or hunger, we can do our part to improve the situation. Ask students to think of ways they can help their community. *(Examples: donate clothes to a shelter, distribute children's books to hospitals, recycle cans and newspapers)*

Learn It & Live It *(page 27)*

Have students work independently to develop their own list of "Ten Commandments of Loving Yourself." Then divide class into small groups and have students negotiate a final list of ten commandments based on their individual responses. Invite each group to share their list with the class and to explain why they think the commandments can help people treat themselves with love and respect.

 ## Family in Action

Students have learned that one aspect of valuing life requires that we take good care of ourselves. Invite students to work with their families to assess and improve the safety of their homes. For example, a family may discover that they need drawer locks for young children, fire extinguishers, or an emergency evacuation plan.

Alternatively, you may invite students to develop a family contract in which each member of the family commits to developing a new habit that can improve his or her health and the other family members promise to provide support. For example, one person might commit to exercising three times a week and the other family members to helping that person make the time to do so.

You may want to begin the next class by asking students to share how they and their families have put Jewish wisdom into action by increasing the safety of their homes or the health of their bodies.

CHAPTER 3

THE Value OF Free Will

Textbook pages 28–43

Core Concept

Every person is given the gift of free will and is responsible for his or her choices.

Learning Objectives

Students will be able to:

- ❂ Explain the concept of free will by providing examples of choices they have made.
- ❂ Demonstrate an understanding of the impulse to do good, or *yetzer hatov*, and the impulse to do bad, or *yetzer hara*, by comparing and contrasting the two concepts.
- ❂ Discuss Judaism's teaching that it is possible to be a very good person without being perfect by giving examples from the Bible.
- ❂ Choose to take actions that are influenced by their *yetzer hatov*.

Chapter Overview

This chapter teaches that only human beings have free will. Free will enables us to know the difference between right and wrong, and makes us responsible for our actions. No person is perfect, but all of us are capable of much goodness.

Key Vocabulary

Free Will The ability to understand the difference between right and wrong and to choose between them

Yetzer Hara The impulse to do wrong

Yetzer Hatov The impulse to do good

Getting Started: Unpacking the Text
(pages 28–29)

Invite a student to the front of the class to read *Pirkei Avot* 2:9 on page 28. Ask: What is Rabbi Yoḥanan's lesson? *(We learn how to behave by observing the behavior of others, both good and bad. We should use good behavior as our model and avoid bad behavior.)* Ask students to describe good behaviors they learned by observing others. Tell them they can share the names of the people if they so wish. *(Possible answers: parent being caring when child is ill, older sister studying for tests, friend sharing his lunch when student forgot hers at home)* Ask them to describe bad behaviors they learned to avoid by observing others. Tell them they should *not* share the names of the people. *(observed people gossiping or endangering themselves by crossing at a red light or smoking)*

Read aloud the story on page 29, then ask students what the sister meant by "the answer is in your hands". *(It would be the boy's decision whether or not to let the bird live.)* Distribute a sheet of paper to each student. Have students list ten decisions they made yesterday or today. *(brushed teeth, crossed at a green light, did homework, ate a bag of potato chips, played a sport, watched television)* Have students place a check next to the decisions they think were good choices. Have them put an X next to the decisions they think were less good. Invite students to share their choices and to brainstorm what they could do differently next time. Point out that every day we have many opportunities to make new and better choices.

Tell students that in this chapter they will learn about what influences our choices and how to make better choices.

Choices and Impulses *(pages 30–35)*

Create a list of several situations where a choice needs to be made. *(Examples: A student is thirsty but finds a long line at the water fountain. Should the student wait his turn or cut in line? An older sibling received a CD as a gift. Should her younger sister take the CD to school without asking for permission?)* After reading the core text in this section, divide the class into pairs, with one student in each pair taking on the role of the *yetzer hatov* and the second that of the *yetzer hara.*

Assign one situation to each group. One at a time, have each group come to the front of the room and invite the *yetzer hatov* and *yetzer hara* to present the situation and role-play a debate regarding what choice would be the best.

Power and Freedom *(page 30)*

Divide students into small groups. Ask them to read the paragraph and collaborate on developing a possible answer. *(It seems easier to take the evil rather than the good course of action; being bad can be fun.)* Then invite students to develop a scenario in which someone feels tempted to choose evil for the reason they have stated. *(A person is tempted to steal because it seems easier than working for the money. A fourteen-year-old is tempted to drive her parents' car because she thinks it will be fun.)*

Invite each group to present its scenario to the class and to ask their classmates for suggestions on how to resist the temptation to do evil and to make a good decision instead.

Bible Bio and Extraordinary Acts *(page 33)*

Invite volunteers to read aloud these two features. Then ask the class how Rebecca might have been a role model for Lillian Wald. *(Rebecca shared the resource of water. Her generosity might have inspired Lillian Wald to share her financial resources. Rebecca responded to someone in physical need. Her concern might have inspired Lillian Wald to become a nurse to help people in physical need.)* Ask: How can these women be role models for you?

A Bad Habit *(page 34)*

Invite students to work individually or in small, collaborative learning groups to answer the question, and then have them share their answers with the class.

Ooh It's So Tempting *(page 35)*

Possible answers: considering the consequences of my actions, walking away from temptation, spending time with people who help me make good choices

People Can Be Like Fire *(page 35)*

Have students share their answers to the first question. *(Possible answers: We would be robotic. We would not have the opportunity to become better people because all our actions would be preprogrammed.)*

We Are Imperfect but Good *(pages 36–38)*

Have each student create a family paper chain of goodness. Provide the students with several pieces of light-colored construction paper, scissors, markers, and staplers. Ask students to cut construction paper into strips. Instruct each student to first write his or her own name on one strip of paper and then write the names of close family members on the other strips (one per person). On each strip with a name, have the student write the person's relationship to him or her *(myself, father, sister)* and an action that person has taken that reflects his or her goodness; for example, "Joan—sister—volunteers at the food bank."

Instruct students to staple their strips into chains. Invite students to share their chains with the class.

Come Down to Earth *(page 37)*

Your students may enjoy role-playing a television talk show based on this Hasidic story. Invite students to play the roles of the program host, Rabbi Moshe, and the angel. The remaining students can be studio audience members who are invited to pose their own questions at the end of the interview. Sample questions posed by the host or audience might include: Rabbi, do you think it's easy to be an angel? Angel, what do you think you would enjoy about living on earth? What do you think would be difficult? If time allows, permit a second set of students to role-play the host, rabbi, and angel.

A Minyan of Thieves *(page 38)*

Have students work individually or with a partner to answer the question. Invite them to share their responses with the class. Explain that our sages teach that being part of a crowd does not remove individual responsibility.

Invite students to describe situations in which others tried to persuade them to do what they knew was wrong—for example, smoke a cigarette or pay for one admission at the movies but sneak into a second show. Encourage students to share how they resisted the peer pressure to make a bad decision and to offer helpful suggestions for others.

Teaching Enrichment: We Are Responsible for Our Choices

(pages 39–41)

Invite students to debate whether or not a wrong behavior can ever be a right choice. For example, are there times when breaking the law is the right choice? *(Yes: to save a human life; the Underground Railroad depended on people breaking the law to save lives and grant freedom to others. No: no one is above the law; rather than break the law, work to change it.)* You may want to invite the rabbi to participate in this discussion.

 **Photo Op** *(page 40)*

Point out to your students that we may not always feel like wearing a helmet when we ride a scooter or bike, but the voice of our *yetzer hatov* reminds us that it's the right thing to do. Then ask: What other actions might you prefer not to take but do take because you hear the voice of your *yetzer hatov?*

Ancient Stories for Modern Times *(page 41)*

Have students read the story as a class or in small, collaborative learning groups. Invite them to share their answers with the class. Ask students to give modern examples of "shortcuts." *(littering, purchasing an illegally made DVD, copying a friend's homework)* What does the Talmud teach about such shortcuts? *(They are wrong regardless of how many people did it before you.)*

 Family in Action

Encourage students to discuss with their parents some of the good choices that are hard for them to make on a daily basis, such as doing their homework before watching television, walking and feeding the family pet, or waking up on time for school. Encourage students to discuss why it is so difficult for them to make those choices. Brainstorm as a class what the benefits are of making each good choice.

You may also suggest that they draw on a piece of paper a circle for each good choice, write the choice inside the circle, and then draw sun rays on the outside. Along each ray students can write the name of a person who benefits from that good decision. For example, by getting up on time for school, the student benefits because he or she is able to avoid family upset and get to school on time. The student's parents benefit because it reduces stress. Car pool members or students on the school bus also benefit because they're not delayed.

Encourage students to ask their parents for suggestions and support to help them increase the frequency with which they make good choices. Invite students to keep a chart for a week or two to track if they are able to make those good choices more frequently. Students may want to share the results of this family activity with the class.

THE VALUE OF FREE WILL

CHAPTER 4

THE Value OF Persistence

Textbook pages 44–55

Core Concept
We must all persist in doing our part to make the world a better place.

Learning Objectives
Students will be able to:
- Describe how their growing knowledge and persistence enable them to take specific actions that add goodness to the world.
- Explain why no one person or generation can complete the work of improving the world.
- Identify actions they can take to contribute to meeting long-term communal goals.

Chapter Overview
This chapter teaches the value of persistence in our efforts to help fulfill the Covenant. It teaches how persistence can help us work through challenges that arise when we attempt difficult tasks. Persistence helps us grow throughout our lives and become increasingly competent.

Key Vocabulary
Persistence The capacity to continue making an effort despite difficulties that arise in achieving a goal

 ## Getting Started: Unpacking the Text
(pages 44–45)

Invite a student to read *Pirkei Avot* 2:16 on page 44. Ask: To what does "work" refer? *(the efforts to make the world a better place; for example, feeding the hungry, curing disease, helping the elderly)* Why isn't it your duty to complete the work? *(There is too much for one person to do.)* Why are we not free to stop trying? *(The only way we can succeed in improving the world is if we all continue to do our part.)*

Pirkei Avot 2:16 provides the lyrics for a popular Hebrew song. If there is time, you may want to ask your cantor or music specialist to teach the song to your class.

Read aloud the story on page 45 to your students. Ask students to describe how they think the Israelites felt as they wandered through the Sinai wilderness. *(frustrated, angry, tired, impatient, frightened)* Write their responses on the chalkboard, then select volunteers to role-play the story. Ask the volunteers to imagine what the Israelites might have said to one another.

After a few minutes, invite two additional volunteers to play the roles of the good impulse—the *yetzer hatov*—and the evil impulse—the *yetzer hara*. Ask them to respectively encourage or discourage the Israelites to persist in their journey to the Promised Land. (You may want to refresh students' memories of what they learned in Chapter 3, "The Value of Free Will.")

Tell your students that in this chapter they will learn why Judaism stresses the value of persistence.

Just Keep on Keepin' On *(page 46)*

Hang a poster-size piece of butcher-block paper on the chalkboard. Draw a large circle to represent each student in your class. One at a time, invite students to write their name in one of the circles and to list a goal they were able to achieve because they were persistent. *(learned to play a musical instrument, scored a soccer goal, learned to read Hebrew)* When all the students have filled in their circles, point out that everyone in the class has experience in overcoming difficulties by being persistent. Invite students to describe some of the difficulties they had to overcome to achieve their goals.

Photo Op *(page 46)*

After students respond to the question in the caption, distribute a piece of paper to each student. Ask them to list every person who has helped them learn to read Hebrew and every grade in which they have studied Hebrew, and to try to figure out the total number of hours spent studying Hebrew. Then ask: How many students learned the *alef bet* and to read Hebrew with the help of one person in an hour? two hours? three hours? Discuss why it is helpful to be patient and realistic when trying to meet challenging goals. *(helps you to avoid becoming discouraged and giving up)*

One Life, Many Opportunities *(pages 46–50)*

Invite volunteers to read aloud one line each from *Pirkei Avot* 5:21 on page 47, starting with "At five years,...." Then divide your class into small groups and ask each group to develop its own list of purposes and strengths for that same age range of five to eighty years. Invite groups to share their lists with the class. Discuss what purposes and strengths of the age closest to their own students most value. What purposes and strengths do students most look forward to developing? Finally, invite them to discuss the purposes and strengths that can help them contribute to fulfilling the Covenant and why they would be valuable.

Bible Bio *(page 48)* and Extraordinary Acts *(page 49)*

After they have read these two features, engage students in a discussion of whether or not they think that persistence is an important quality for a leader to have. Ask them to explain why they think it is or isn't.

It's My Goal *(page 51)*

Have students read and work through this activity individually. Ask them to share their goals. Are they surprised that some classmates have similar goals? Are they surprised that some have very different goals from one another? Why or why not?

Teaching Enrichment: It's My Goal *(page 51)*

Ask: Is it ever acceptable to give up on or change a goal? *(No: Once you commit to a goal, you must persevere until you achieve it. Yes: Our goals can change; for example, someone may want to be a concert pianist but realize after three years of lessons that he or she has other interests and talents, and decide instead just to be a good amateur pianist.)*

Artist's Corner: A Job for Many Generations *(pages 50–54)*

Distribute a sheet of light-colored construction paper and markers to each student. Have each student write his or her name at the top of the paper and draw a large circle below the name. Then have the students divide their circles into a pie chart with four equal parts. Ask students to label each of the four sections of their pie chart with a *mitzvah* for improving the world *(for example, caring for animals, planting a garden, donating tzedakah, pursuing justice)* and to illustrate the four *mitzvot*.

Invite students to tape their papers on the wall. Have students indicate their interest in participating in up to two *mitzvot* listed on each of their classmates' pie charts by initialing the outer rim of that *mitzvah*. If there are *mitzvot* without initials, ask the class to brainstorm ways to recruit others to participate; for example, by putting a notice in the synagogue bulletin.

As a class, review all the *mitzvot* that are listed and see what actions your students can take to contribute to their fulfillment.

Let Us Begin *(page 52)*

Invite students to share their answers and then ask them how they feel about working on a task they may never see completed. For example, their actions may help add peace to the world, but students themselves may not live to see the world completely at peace. Ask students what they think motivates others to contribute their part to tasks that take many generations to complete. *(Possible answers: They are trying to do their part to fulfill the Covenant. They care about future generations. It makes them feel good to do good.)* Then invite the class to read "The Carob Tree" on page 53.

Ancient Stories for Modern Times *(page 53)*

After students have read the story and completed the activity, invite them to share their answers. Ask them what might have motivated adults in their community to raise money to build schools, playgrounds, or a children's museum despite the fact that they themselves were too old to benefit from them. *(They had children or grand-children who would benefit; it was their way of saying thank you to people who had provided for them when they were young.)* Encourage students to think of what they would like to provide the next generation. *(Possible answers: a youth lounge in the synagogue, a public garden, computers for the religious school)*

Learn It & Live It *(page 55)*

Invite students to share their answers. Focus students on how their religious school experiences and studies can help them succeed in making contributions to the larger world. *(Working on tzedakah projects can teach students teamwork and organizational skills, and help them develop leadership skills. Studying such Jewish values as honesty, kindness, and peace can help them learn to value themselves and others, make good choices, and persist when a task is challenging.)*

 **Family in Action**

After reading the last section in the chapter ("A Job for Many Generations," pages 50–54), invite students to consider how they can contribute to a task that will make the world a better place but requires more than one person or one generation to complete it; for example, creating a peaceful or just world. Some activities students may consider are: working in a shelter for the homeless, visiting a nursing home, or running a synagogue-wide winter coat drive.

You can either develop a class project that involves students' families or encourage students and their families to choose their own projects. What is important is that students understand the value of living Rabbi Tarfon's lesson (see page 44 of the textbook)—doing their part even though they cannot complete the entire task.

Encourage students to share what they did and how it felt to do their part.

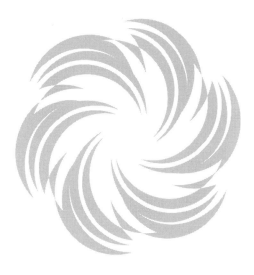

CHAPTER 5

THE Value OF Study

Textbook pages 56–69

Core Concept

The Torah provides us with the instructions for living rewarding and meaningful lives. The Jewish people cannot survive without the study of Torah.

Learning Objectives

Students will be able to:

- Explain why we continue to study Torah throughout our lives.
- Provide examples of how the Torah's instructions can be practically applied to modern life.
- Discuss why the Jewish people cannot survive without the study of Torah.

Chapter Overview

This chapter teaches that we continue to study Torah throughout our lives to deepen our understanding of its instructions. Students learn how the ancient wisdom of the Torah and our sages can be applied to the modern world, and how the study of Torah helps the Jewish people survive.

Key Vocabulary

Bikur Ḥolim The mitzvah of visiting the sick

Kibud Av Va'eim The mitzvah of honoring one's parents

Parashah Weekly portion of the Torah that is read in the synagogue

Sidra Alternative name for the weekly portion of the Torah that is read in the synagogue

Talmud Torah The study of Torah

Getting Started: Unpacking the Text

(pages 56–57)

Invite a volunteer to read aloud *Pirkei Avot* 5:22 on page 56. Say to the students, "I am thinking of a small object that you hold up to your eyes and turn; each time you turn it you see something new and different. What is it?" *(a kaleidoscope)* If possible, bring in a kaleidoscope and ask each of your students to look through the eyepiece. (For health reasons, tell students not to put the kaleidoscope right up to their eyes.) Ask students what they think Ben Bag-Bag (pronounced *Bahg-Bahg*) might have meant when he spoke of turning the Torah again and again. *(Read it again and again.)* Then ask students how reading the Torah again and again might be like looking through a kaleidoscope. *(Each time you read it you see something new in it.)*

Read aloud the story on page 57 or invite several students to do so. Ask: Why does the story teach that their children (and all generations of children after them) were what was most precious to the Israelites? *(because the children could study Torah and therefore know how to fulfill God's commandments and the* Brit*)*

Tell students that in this chapter they will learn why the Jewish people value the study of Torah above all else.

Instructions, Please! *(pages 58–60)*

Before reading the text, invite students to share a favorite story or lesson from the Torah. Ask them why they like the story or lesson and if it has influenced them in any way or has added to their pride in being Jewish.

The World's First Torah in Outer Space *(page 58)*

Ask: What Jewish possession would you bring on a long journey? Invite students to explain their choices. Then ask students how they feel knowing that an astronaut brought a Torah scroll aboard a space shuttle and read from it while orbiting above Jerusalem.

 Photo Op *(page 60)*

Ask: How can a computer such as the one at the top of the page be used to reach out to people in need? *(Possible answers: e-mail a greeting card and homework assignments to a sick friend, find out how to help people after a natural disaster strikes)* Invite students to think of how other modern conveniences, such as, jets and cell phones can be used to help those in need.

Ask: How can the bicycle and basket in the picture at the bottom of the page be used to fulfill a *mitzvah*? *(Possible answers: deliver groceries to an elderly person, collect children's books from neighbors and donate them to a hospital, bring recyclables to a collection site)* How can other old-fashioned tools, such as a manual food chopper, mops, and paper and pencil, be used to perform *mitzvot*? *(Possible answers: cook a meal for a homebound friend or neighbor, mop an elderly person's floor, write a letter to a soldier overseas or a nursing home resident)*

Teaching Enrichment: Read! Study! Action! *(page 61)*

Tell students that there is public debate about whether or not displays of religious symbols, such as Christmas trees and Ḥanukkah menorahs, should be permitted on public property. Ask students if they think the Ten Commandments should be displayed on public property, such as government buildings? *(Yes: Everyone can agree on these laws; God's teachings should be in as many places as possible. No: Religious teachings and symbols do not belong on government property; this is part of the separation of church and state.)*

Read! Study! Action! *(page 61)*

Ask: What question might you add to those of the heavenly court? *(Possible answers: Did you speak respectfully to others and avoid gossip? Did you set aside tzedakah each week? Did you appreciate the blessings in your life?)*

Older and Wiser *(page 63)*

Invite students to share their answers to the activity. On the chalkboard, list students' answers to the second question. Review the story on page 57 of the textbook. Explain that through their increased knowledge and increased ability to perform *mitzvot*, the students are proving that they are, indeed, the most precious possession of the Jewish people.

Ask students what other areas of Jewish study they would like to learn about. *(how to chant Torah, modern Hebrew, Jewish history, Jewish music)*

Creation 1 and 2 *(page 65)*

Divide class into pairs or collaborative learning groups to discuss and complete this activity. *(Each of us can act in godly ways; for example, by being compassionate and generous*

to those in need. Each of us has a spark of the divine in us that can help us add goodness to the world.)

Throughout the Day *(page 65)*

Have students read and work through this activity individually. Invite students to share their answers. *(Possible answers: Every day can be enriched by the teachings of the Torah. We can talk to our parents about the Bible stories we learn. As we ride or walk to school we can think about the actions that will help us become our best selves. Each morning we have a new opportunity to help fulfill the Covenant.)*

Artist's Corner: Like a Fish out of Water *(page 67)*

Rabbi Akiva used a metaphor to explain the importance of studying Torah. Ask students to create their own metaphors to describe the Jewish people's dependence on Torah. *(Examples: Just as animals need air to live, so the Jewish people need Torah; Just as plants need sunlight....)*

Distribute drawing or construction paper, and markers or crayons. (Alternatively, invite students to create a mural on a large piece of butcher-block paper.) Have students write down and illustrate their metaphors. The artwork can then be displayed on a classroom bulletin board or in a school hallway.

Bible Bio and Extraordinary Acts *(page 68)*

Point out that the Torah teaches that Moses instructed the Israelites about all that God had told him. So, too, Rebecca Gratz worked hard to ensure that this knowledge continues to be passed down from one generation to the next.

Family in Action

Have students each select a story or feature they have read in the textbook, such as "The World's First Torah in Outer Space" on page 58, and invite them to present it at a teach-in to which you invite their families. Students can read aloud the stories or features and briefly discuss the lessons they teach. You can make the event more festive by serving light refreshments and by decorating the room with artwork your students have made. (If you serve refreshments, check what dietary regulations your synagogue observes.)

CHAPTER 6

THE Value OF Community

Textbook pages 70–83

Core Concept

As Jews we are obligated to actively participate in and strengthen our community.

Learning Objectives

Students will be able to:

- Identify the types of communities to which they belong and the purpose of those communities.
- Describe the importance of individual responsibility within a community.
- Provide examples of how praying, studying, and celebrating together help strengthen the Jewish community.
- Take actions to contribute to their religious school community and the broader Jewish community.

Chapter Overview

This chapter explores the importance of participating in Jewish communal life. It presents some of the key ways to be involved with the community; for example, by attending synagogue prayer services, studying in community with others, and celebrating holidays and life-cycle events with one's congregation.

Key Vocabulary

Klal Yisra'el The entire Jewish people; a concept that reflects the unity of the Jewish people

 Getting Started: Unpacking the Text
(pages 70–71)

Invite a volunteer to read *Pirkei Avot* 2:4 on page 70. Ask: Why is it important not to separate oneself from the community? *(By participating in a community you have the opportunity to learn from others, receive from and give to others, and help build a better life for everyone.)*

Before reading the folktale on page 71 do this exercise: Have students stand in a circle at arm's length from one another. Distribute a plastic spoon to each student. Ask students to stretch their hand with the spoon straight out in front of themselves. Finally, tell them to try to "feed" themselves with their spoon without bending their elbows. Of course, they will not succeed. Then instruct your students to keep their hands outstretched and to "feed" the person to their right. Point out that by reaching out to others they also managed to be "fed."

Read and discuss the story. Then tell your students that in this chapter they will learn the value of being an active member of the Jewish community.

Build a Holy Community *(page 72)*

Go around the room and ask students to describe several communities to which they belong *(synagogue, sports team, family, school)* and to describe the purpose of each community. List the communities on the chalkboard. Make sure that at least one student mentions your religious school or synagogue. After each student has had a turn, read each item on the list and ask all the students who are members of that community to stand.

In all likelihood, the only community to which *all* students belong will be your religious school or synagogue. Point out that though there may be many differences among the class

23

members, one thing they have in common is that they are all members of the same religious school community, and that it is a sacred community.

Bible Bio (page 72)

Ask: What might have happened if Moses hadn't listened to Jethro? (*The community would have lost its only judge when Moses died. Moses would not have established a judicial system that would benefit the community for generations after his death.*)

The Extraordinary Acts of Ordinary People (page 73)

Ask students if they are surprised that a teenager was able to inspire so many adults to pursue justice for themselves. Then ask your students to consider what actions they might want to take to inspire others to do good.

Invite students to role-play a scene in which Clara Lemlich rallies other workers to go on strike and some workers resist. Have one student be Lemlich and several students be other workers. Before beginning the role-playing activity, help your students get into their roles by discussing why some workers might initially have resisted going on strike. (*fear of losing their jobs, fear of violence, the hope that change would come about without their having to make an effort*)

We Need One Another (page 73)

Invite students to share their responses. Have students individually or in small groups write a prayer of thanks to God for bringing the people who have helped them into their lives. For example, they might write: Praised are You, Adonai our God, Ruler of the world, who blessed me with the goodness of knowing (insert names of people). Alternatively, students can begin their blessing with the traditional Hebrew words, *Baruch atah Adonai, Eloheinu melech ha'olam,* and continue in English.

We Study as a Community (pages 73–74)

Ask your students to list the benefits of studying with their religious school class-mates. (*meet new friends, learn from others, share what we know*)

We Pray as a Community (page 75)

Bring prayer books to class and show your students examples of prayers that use the communal voice. Examples are Shalom Rav (*Siddur Sim Shalom, 1998,* page 44; *Gates of Prayer,* 1975, page 46; *Kol Haneshamah,* 1994, page 105) and the prayer recited before studying Torah (*Siddur Sim Shalom, 1998,* page 63; *Gates of Prayer,* 1975, page 52; *Kol Haneshamah,* 1994, page 169). You may also invite your students to search the prayer book for other examples of prayers that are written in the communal voice.

Artist's Corner: We Support Each Other as a Community

(page 76)

Speak to your educational director or rabbi and find out who in the community is elderly, homebound, or hospitalized and would appreciate receiving a greeting card from your students. Try to find out enough information about each person so that your students can develop a sense of who the people are. Invite students to select a person for whom they want to create a card. Distribute drawing or construction paper and other art supplies, such as markers, foil, glue, and crayons, with which to create the cards.

Before they begin illustrating the cards, have students fold their papers in half or quarters and write an appropriate message on the inside portion of the card. This may be a good opportunity to invite your rabbi to speak to your class about the mitzvah of visiting the sick, *bikur ḥolim.*

Can You Be Part of the Jewish Community yet Different? *(pages 77–78)*

Distribute a sheet of paper to each student. Ask students to write the name of every member of the class on their paper, skipping a line between each name. Then ask them to write one positive, nonphysical quality about each person. *(Jonathan is loyal, Nina is smart, Jocelyn is funny, Adam is generous)* Collect all the papers. Take them home and collate all the comments so that you have one sheet of paper for each student with all the comments about him or her on that paper.

Read the comments aloud the next time your class meets and then give each student the paper with the comments about him or her. Point out to students that they each have many different strengths and good points, and that together they form a strong and supportive community.

Ancient Stories for Modern Times *(page 79)*

What might God request of us that would require us to work patiently together? *(Possible answers: create a wildlife sanctuary for animals, help feed and clothe the needy, care for the sick, help free people who are oppressed, work to increase peace in the world)* How might being persistent help us succeed? *(Each of these tasks is challenging; persistence would help us keep trying even when we were tired or frustrated.)*

 ## Artist's Corner: Make a Difference as a Community

(pages 80–82)

Invite students to portray Rav Yirmiyah's teaching that a person who works to meet the needs of the community is like one who is occupied with Torah (see page 81 of the textbook). Distribute drawing or construction paper and crayons or markers. (If you prefer, students can work together on a mural using butcher-block paper.) Have students draw the outline of an open Torah scroll with the *etzim* (roller handles of wood) on the sides. Inside the Torah scroll, ask students to draw their visions of how they can help meet the needs of the community. Students' work can make a nice classroom or hallway display.

 ## Teaching Enrichment: Make a Difference as a Community
(pages 80–82)

Invite students to discuss the core concept that we are obligated to participate in and strengthen our community. Ask: Can we choose not to participate? *(Yes: We have free will and can choose not to participate; the community is not a priority in my life; others have made the community a priority, so they can do the work. No: We have an obligation to honor our Covenant with God by working with others to improve the world; to benefit from a community's strengths requires that we also accept the challenges of that community and work toward improving it.)*

Increased Responsibility *(page 81)*

Why does Judaism teach that we have increased responsibilities to a community the longer we live in it? *(The longer we live in a community, the more we benefit from what it has to offer, so the more we should contribute to it.)* Ask: What services does our town or city provide for all of us? *(public library, public schools, parks, gardens, police and fire departments)* How are these services paid for and supported? *(by taxes that the citizens pay and donations of people's time and money)* What would happen if people refused to give their time and money? *(Eventually these services would no longer be available or only wealthy people could afford them.)*

 ## Photo Op *(page 82)*

How is supporting the Jewish homeland, Israel, like being "occupied with Torah"? *(The Torah teaches that it is a mitzvah to love Israel. When we support Israel by visiting the Jewish homeland, giving tzedakah, or planting trees in Israel, we are honoring this sacred teaching.)*

 ## Family in Action

You may want to take this opportunity to build community among your students' families. Consider inviting the families to class for a social experience—listening to Israeli music, learning about an upcoming holiday, or watching a movie with Jewish content followed by a discussion of the movie. Begin by welcoming your guests and inviting everyone to introduce him- or herself. You can make the event more festive by serving light refreshments. (If you serve refreshments, check what dietary regulations your synagogue observes.)

CHAPTER 7

THE Value OF Judging

Textbook pages 84–95

Core Concept

We are commanded to pursue justice for ourselves and for others. When judging others we must balance justice with mercy.

Learning Objectives

Students will be able to:

- Articulate the reasons for tempering justice with mercy.
- Explain by example the value of rebuke and describe Maimonides' guidelines.
- Make increasingly sound judgments based on reliable evidence, fairness, honesty, and humility.

Chapter Overview

This chapter teaches that making judgments is part of our daily lives. It teaches that we must gather and evaluate evidence, judge fairly and honestly, consider what we would have done in a similar circumstance, and temper justice with mercy. It also teaches that sometimes we must rebuke someone for their actions but that it should be done with sensitivity and respect, for the person's own good.

Key Vocabulary

Tocheiḥah Rebuke or reprimand
Tzedek Justice

 ## Getting Started: Unpacking the Text

(pages 84–85)

Invite a student to read *Pirkei Avot* 2:4 on page 84. Ask students to explain Hillel's lesson in their own words. *(Before making a judgment about someone, think about what you would do in a similar circumstance.)*

Invite a student to the front of the class to read the story on page 85. Explain to students that the biblical punishment for murder was execution. To avoid executing an innocent person, the Talmud does not permit the acceptance of circumstantial, or indirect, evidence; for example, seeing a bloodied weapon in a person's hand. For someone to be found guilty of murder, the testimony of at least two eyewitnesses is required.

Ask students to brainstorm a scenario in which the accused man ran into the shop with the sword in his hand, was later found holding the sword dripping with blood, but did not commit the murder. *(He ran after the victim to warn him that someone in the shop wanted to kill him. He was going to use the sword to defend the victim. In the shop the murderer pulled the sword out of the accused man's hand and stabbed the victim. The accused man removed the sword from the victim's body in the hope that he could save his life. Witnesses arrived just as the accused man was about to drop the knife and try to revive the victim.)*

Tell your students that in this chapter they will learn about the value of justice and the importance of carefully gathering and evaluating evidence.

 ## Teaching Enrichment: Getting Started

(page 85)

Invite your students to challenge the rabbinic ruling in the story on page 85. You may choose to invite your rabbi to participate in the discussion. Ask: Do you think justice was served? *(Yes: The accused may have been innocent; justice isn't served by executing or imprisoning the innocent. No: There was enough circumstantial evidence to conclude the man was guilty.)* Does the Talmud demand too strong a burden of proof by requiring eyewitnesses to a murder? *(Yes: As a result, criminals can go free. No: It's more important that innocent lives be saved than that all murders be punished.)*

 Artist's Corner: Try on Their Shoes *(pages 86–87)*

Distribute construction paper and crayons or pencils to each student. Have students trace the outline of one of their shoes on the paper. Then invite them to write at least five brief, nonphysical facts about themselves *(plays soccer, attends religious school, loves math and music)* on the shoeprint. The more details they record, the more unique their shoeprints.

Collect the shoeprints and randomly redistribute them, one per student. Ask: Do you know whose shoeprint you have? Invite each student to read a shoeprint aloud and identify its owner. If a student does not correctly guess the person being described, permit other students to guess. After each shoeprint is correctly matched with a student, ask students: What have you learned about (name of student)? Have you discovered something you have in common with (name)? Have you learned something that surprises you?

Bible Bio *(page 89)*

Ask: Why do you think the daughters of Tz'lafeḥad took their case to Moses? *(Possible answers: The issue was so important that Moses himself, not a lower judge, needed to decide the case. The daughters wanted a decision that would not be appealed.)* Ask: What did Moses do after hearing the case? *(Moses sought the answer from God.)* In the end, who decided the case? *(God)*

The Extraordinary Acts of Ordinary People *(page 90)*

Have three volunteers read aloud one paragraph each. Ask students how they feel knowing that a United States Supreme Court justice attended religious school, just as they are doing, and that she keeps a quote from the Torah posted on her wall. Ask how they think remaining in religious school through confirmation might have helped Justice Ginsburg succeed professionally *(Possible answers: Continuing to study Torah helped her develop a love of justice. It taught her persistence. It inspired her to help the community.)*

Ancient Stories for Modern Times *(page 91)*

Have students read the story to themselves or in small groups, then invite them to role-play the story. Assign individual students to be the beggar, the rich person, and the judge. The rest of the class can be the jury. Have jury members ask each person to state his or her position and to explain if justice was served. Afterward, invite students to suggest an alternative ending. *(The judge decided that the beggar had to repay the loan but required the townspeople to employ him so that he could earn the money to repay it.)*

**Photo Op** (page 92, bottom)

Ask students why they think the sign asks "What was the *kindest* thing anybody did for you today?" rather than "What kind thing did somebody do for you today?" (*On any given day many kind things are done for us—people may hold doors for us, drive us to school, compliment how we look, and help us with our homework. If we don't pay attention, we may take people's kindness for granted.*)

The Value of Rebuke (page 93)

Possible answers: Perhaps Maimonides thought that although justice may require us to rebuke someone, we also must be merciful because Judaism teaches us to treat others with respect and concern, as we would want to be treated. Rebuking someone for his or her own good shows caring, doing so in private spares the person public embarrassment, and speaking gently, with concern, is respectful.

Family in Action

Invite students to share with their families what they have learned about putting themselves in someone else's shoes, pursuing justice, and balancing justice with mercy. Encourage students to discuss at home how they can implement these Jewish values within their family. Invite students to share the results with the class.

CHAPTER 8 | THE Value OF Possessions

Textbook pages 96–107

Core Concepts

Our tradition encourages us to fulfill our physical and emotional needs and to take pleasure in life. But it also asks us to set reasonable limits on our self-fulfillment and pleasure seeking so that we act responsibly and with concern for the people and world around us.

Learning Objectives

Students will be able to:

☼ Provide examples in Jewish tradition that illustrate a balance between a person's physical and spiritual needs.

☼ Distinguish between their needs and their desires.

☼ Explain how contributing tzedakah adds justice to the world.

Chapter Overview

This chapter explores the importance of learning to balance personal needs and desires with the needs of others. It helps students explore the question of how many possessions—clothing, jewelry, computer games, CDs—are enough for them. And it guides students to an understanding of how they can enjoy what they have and share with others.

Key Vocabulary

Avodah Worship, work

Tzedakah A just action; usually a reference to a donation to a charitable cause

 ## Getting Started: Unpacking the Text

(pages 96–97)

Invite a volunteer to read *Pirkei Avot* 3:7 on page 96. Ask: What does this verse teach us? (*Everything in Creation belongs to God, not to humans; all blessings in our lives come from God.*)

Bring to class a small piece of glass (it can be something as simple as a clear drinking glass) and a mirror. One at a time, invite each student to look at the other members of the class through the glass and then to hold the mirror in front of him- or herself. Ask students what they saw and record their answers on the board. Then ask students how they might feel if they could see only themselves. How might they feel if they could never see themselves?

Choose three students to come to the front of the class to read aloud the story on page 97. Ask one student to read the part of the narrator, another the part of the rabbi, and the third the part of Mendel. After the students have role-played the story, invite two other students to portray the rabbi and Mendel, and to role-play a conversation that continues the story. Say to the student who is portraying Mendel, "How might you answer the rabbi?" If there is time, you may want to select another pair of students to continue the role playing.

Tell students that in this chapter they will learn about the value of enjoying and sharing their possessions.

Let's Be Practical *(pages 98–99)*

Divide the class into small groups of two to three students. Ask each group to teach Rabbi Elazar ben Azaryah's lesson using a different example in place of food, such as water, air or shelter. Have one student from each group write its example on the chalkboard. Have students explain how their statement teaches Rabbi Azaryah's lesson.

Ancient Stories for Modern Times *(page 99)*

Have students work individually, in pairs, or in small groups to complete the activity. Ask: Why were Rabbi Shimon and his sons reprimanded? *(Because they reprimanded the Jewish farmers for doing what the Torah teaches—raising food in order to sustain life.)* Why were they blamed for trying to destroy the world? *(Because after they condemned the farmers, the fields were covered in flames as a punishment; if the farmers had followed their advice they wouldn't have produced the food that is necessary for life.)* Why were they told to go back to the cave? *(They had not learned the lessons of Torah that teach the importance of sustaining life.)*

Did You Know? *(page 100)*

Invite the class to brainstorm ways in which the two meanings of *avodah*—"worship" and "work"—can be connected. *(Possible answer: When we work to keep ourselves healthy or to help someone in need it is as if we are worshipping God because we are caring for one of God's creations. When we work to conserve natural resources, such as water, gasoline, and heating oil, it is as if we are worshipping God because we are acting as nature's guardian.)* Write the responses on the chalkboard to help stimulate students' creativity as they complete this activity.

Artist's Corner: How Much Is Enough? *(pages 101–103)*

Bring one or more copies of a Passover Haggadah to class as a resource. Ask students if they are familiar with the hymn "Dayeinu," which is sung at the Passover seder. Explain that *dayeinu* means "it would have been enough" and that the hymn praises God and acknowledges that God has given us more than we need.

In the spirit of "Dayeinu," invite students to create a five-line hymn acknowledging the abundance in their lives. An example is shown below.

> *If we had only food and not candy,* dayeinu, *it would have been enough.*
> *If we had only televisions and not computers,* dayeinu, *it would have been enough.*
> *If we had only schoolyards to play in and not parks,* dayeinu, *it would have been enough.*
> *If we had only loving families and not caring friends,* dayeinu, *it would have been enough.*
> *If we had only good health and not good humor,* dayeinu, *it would have been enough.*

Have students work individually so their hymns can be shared at home and perhaps even used at a Passover seder. You may want to invite each student to contribute one line of his or her hymn to a class "Dayeinu" to be recited at a model or community seder.

Alternatively, create a bulletin board display of students' hymns. Distribute construction paper and art supplies and glue. Invite each student to mount a copy of his or her hymn onto the construction paper and to illustrate it.

Needs Versus Wants *(page 102)*

While students work on the activity, write each of the items listed in the activity on the chalkboard, e.g., "Food," "Sleep," "Love." When students have finished, tally

the responses: For each item, ask for a show of hands to indicate how many students had an "N" and how many a "W." Encourage them to express the reasons for their responses. Ask students what the final tally tells them about the class's priorities.

To Have and to Give *(page 103)*

Divide the class into pairs or small groups and give each a sheet of writing paper. Have students fold the paper twice (along the width and then along the length) to form four quadrants. Using one section for each type of person, have students create a written description of an action that might be taken by an average person *(Nina showed Emily her new pen and returned the one she had borrowed from Emily)*, an uneducated person *(Joe planned to take home the lifeguard's elevated chair and have the lifeguard take his beach chair)*, a saintly person *(Jonathan gave his sister his birthday presents and asked for nothing in return)*, and a wicked person *(After eating her portion of cake, Joy ate her brother's)*.

Invite students to read aloud their descriptions (all four, or one or two descriptions per child), and have their classmates guess the type of person they were describing.

What Do You Think? *(page 104)*

Have students read and work through this activity individually. *(Possible answers: Our tradition requires everyone, including the poor, to give tzedakah because everyone is responsible for adding justice to the world. Finding something of value to contribute to others helps add dignity to the poor person's life.)*

Create Balance *(page 104)*

Ask: Do you think our sages were wise to establish guidelines for tzedakah? *(Yes: The guidelines help ensure that everyone gives a reasonable amount but that people don't impoverish themselves. No: We have free will and therefore should make these decisions ourselves.)*

 ## Teaching Enrichment: A Holy Purpose in Not Believing in God

(page 106)

Ask: Do you agree with Rabbi Moshe Leib that "everything in Creation has a purpose"? *(No: There is no purpose to acts of violence, deadly storms, or diseases that cause people and animals to suffer or die. Yes: People may suffer when bad things happen, but such occasions provide us with an opportunity to behave as creatures made in God's image by helping those who suffer.)*

 ## Family in Action

Develop item 3 in the "Learn It & Live It" activity on page 107 into a class project. Invite your students' families to participate. For example, enlist parents and siblings as helpers to assist in the boxing and dropping off of the items.

CHAPTER 9

THE Value OF Argument

Textbook pages 108–117

Core Concept

Disagreements have the potential to add goodness to the world. Constructive disagreements increase understanding between people, build trust, and bring people closer to the truth; destructive disagreements decrease understanding and trust, and fail to bring people closer to the truth.

Learning Objectives

Students will be able to:

❋ Differentiate between constructive and destructive disagreement.

❋ Explain how an argument can honor God.

❋ Participate in a constructive argument.

Chapter Overview

This chapter teaches students how to harness the potential of constructive disagreements by learning to argue "for the sake of Heaven (God)." Emphasis is put on cultivating the good impulse (*yetzer hatov*), respectfully listening to others, and showing respect and sensitivity when responding to others.

Key Vocabulary

L'sheim shamayim For the sake of Heaven (God)

Minyan A group of ten adult worshippers required for a Jewish prayer service

Getting Started: Unpacking the Text

(pages 108–109)

Ask students if they think it's ever important to disagree with someone. *(No: It's not polite and makes people angry. Yes: It's important to say what you think and feel.)*

Invite a volunteer to read *Pirkei Avot* 5:17 on page 108. Ask students what they think a "disagreement for the sake of honoring God" means. *(a disagreement that is for the sake of figuring out the truth about religion or defending Judaism's teachings)* Explain that a disagreement that is for the sake of honoring God is one in which people add holiness to the world by treating others with respect and seeking knowledge of the truth. Ask students why a disagreement for the sake of honoring God leads to a permanent result, or lasting value, but that one that is not for the sake of honoring God doesn't. *(Respect and truth have lasting value; disrespect and the failure to seek truth do not.)*

Read aloud the story on page 109. Ask students what the story has in common with *Pirkei Avot* 5:17 *(Both teach that disagreement can be a good thing when it leads to learning.)*

Tell students that in this chapter they will learn why and how an argument can be beneficial.

Why Disagree? *(page 110)*

After students have read this section, invite them to discuss how they resolve disagreements with friends. Encourage students to discuss the strategies they use; for example, speaking respectfully and honestly, listening to what the other person has to say, cooling off before they speak, and compromising.

Artist's Corner: Argue for the Sake of Honoring God

(pages 110–114)

After your students have completed this section, review the computer club scenario described on pages 111–112 of the textbook. Have students recap what made the first student's disagreement destructive but the second student's constructive. Then distribute large sheets of drawing or construction paper and markers, colored pencils, or crayons. Invite students to illustrate a four- or five-cell comic strip that presents a *constructive* disagreement, perhaps between siblings, a parent and child, or friends.

Invite students to present their completed artwork to the class. If there is time, you can invite students to role-play one another's comics. You may want to hang the completed strips around the room.

The Destruction of the Second Temple *(page 112)*

Ask: What might be examples of "causeless love"? *(Sharing with others who have not shared with you, speaking politely despite someone else's rudeness, going out of your way to help someone who has ignored you)*

 Photo Op *(page 113)*

Ask students why they think the sign is written in several languages. *(It enables more people to understand the warning.)* Point out that in a disagreement we must use language that the other person can understand. We might need to explain our position in more than one way and more than one time. But no matter how many ways we choose to phrase what we say, our words and tone must remain respectful.

 Teaching Enrichment: Bible Bio *(page 114)*

After students read the text, ask: On whose behalf was Abraham arguing? *(the innocent people who may have lived in Sodom and Gomorrah)* Ask students whether it was appropriate for Abraham to argue with God. *(Yes: You should always stand up for what is just; God may have been testing Abraham to see if he was compassionate and willing to pursue justice for the innocent people. No: There is no greater wisdom than God's; we should never question God's wisdom.)*

You may want to turn back to the daughters of Tz'lafeḥad "Bible Bio" on page 89 of the textbook. Just as Abraham argued with God, so did Maḥlah, Noah, Ḥoglah, Milkah, and Tirtzah disagree with God's instructions. (God instructed Moses to divide the land among the men of the community.) God listened to the daughters of Tz'lafeḥad and agreed that it was just for them to inherit the land that was due their father. Ask students what lesson the text teaches. *(It's important to pursue justice—for yourself or for others—even if it means questioning God.)*

The Extraordinary Acts of Ordinary People (page 115)

Invite three students to each read one paragraph. Ask: How is Bella Abzug a model for arguments that are *l'sheim shamayim*? *(Abzug argued for the sake of adding justice, compassion, and truth to the world. As an attorney she represented and argued on behalf of people who were denied civil liberties; in Congress, she argued for child care and supported Israel.)* How might Abraham have been a role model for Bella Abzug? *(Like Abraham, Abzug argued for justice on behalf of those who did not have the same access to power and authority that she had.)* How can Bella Abzug be a role model for you?

Ancient Stories for Modern Times (page 116)

Invite volunteers to read aloud the text. Have students complete this activity individually or in small groups. Share the responses with the class. *(Possible answers: Having given the Torah to the Jewish people, God wants us to study Torah and interpret its meaning for ourselves. People must work through their disagreements among themselves rather than asking God to create supernatural miracles to prove them right.)*

To help students appreciate the value Judaism places on respectful argumentation, invite them to compare this story with Abraham's "Bible Bio" on textbook page 114. You may also want them to compare the story with Tz'lafeḥad's daughters' "Bible Bio" on textbook page 89. Ask students what the stories have in common. *(Our tradition's teaching that people can respectfully question God's judgment or disagree with God, and God listens to what they have to say)*

Learn It & Live It (page 117)

Invite students to share their responses to item 1. *(speak respectfully, listen to the other person, remain calm, don't interrupt, compromise)* List students' ideas on the chalkboard. Encourage students to develop new strategies and techniques for arguing constructively by using what they have learned from their classmates.

Family in Action

Suggest that students discuss the concepts of constructive and destructive disagreements with their families and share the rules they and their classmates developed for arguing constructively. Ask students to invite their families to add their ideas to the list and to brainstorm how everyone can remember to follow those rules. For example, the list can be posted on the refrigerator; if someone uses the "time out" signal in the middle of a disagreement, everyone needs to pause and consult the list.

Invite students to share their families' ideas as well as their experiences in putting the strategies and techniques into action.

CHAPTER 10

THE Value OF Peace

Textbook pages 118–129

Core Concept

Judaism teaches us to love and seek peace in every aspect of our lives.

Learning Objectives

Students will be able to:

- Explain the extended meaning of *shalom* beyond that of "the absence of war."
- Identify prayers in the siddur that reflect the Jewish tradition of loving and pursuing peace and peacemaking.
- Take actions to pursue peace for others and for themselves.

Chapter Overview

This chapter teaches that according to Jewish tradition, the world cannot be whole until all God's creatures live in peace and safety, nor can any one of us enjoy complete peace of mind and heart until peace reigns for all. Making peace includes not only settling arguments but also providing for the health, food, and shelter of those in need.

Key Vocabulary

Oseh Shalom Peacemaker; one of God's names

Shalom Peace (absence of war; safety, wholeness, completion, fulfillment, prosperity, health and peace of mind and heart), hello, good-bye

Sh'lom Bayit Peace in the home

Getting Started: Unpacking the Text

(pages 118–119)

Invite a volunteer to read *Pirkei Avot* 1:12 on page 118. You may want to explain that Aaron is traditionally seen as a peacemaker because he pursued peace between Moses and the children of Israel when a rift was created because of the Golden Calf.

Ask: What is the difference between loving peace and pursuing peace? *(To love peace is to value it and to take actions that increase peace; to pursue peace is to aggressively go after it. "Pursuing" implies more initiative, a more proactive role than loving.)* If students question whether loving implies taking action, ask if they would believe parents who said that they love their child but who weren't willing to house and clothe the child or someone who said she loved her pet but who didn't feed it.

Ask students for examples of how they can show their love of peace. *(speak respectfully to parents, be patient with a younger sibling, observe rules of team sports)* Then ask students for examples of how they can pursue peace. *(attend a peace rally, be a peacemaker between friends who are arguing, join an interfaith organization)*

Have students read the story on page 119 in small groups. Ask students why they think that cheering up people who are sad and pursuing peace qualified the men for a special place in the world to come—the world in the days after the Messiah comes. *(The men's actions are unselfish and help make the world a better place; their actions add peace to the world.)*

Tell students that in this chapter they will learn about the value of loving and pursuing peace.

A Tradition of Peace *(pages 120–121)*

Invite a student to read aloud the first paragraphs of this section. You may want to point out that the Amidah prayer

concludes with a reference to God as *Oseh Shalom*, "Peacemaker" *(Siddur Sim Shalom,*
1998, page 120; Gates of Prayer, 1975, page 47; Kol Haneshamah, 1994, page 323).

Ask: If one of God's names is *Oseh Shalom* and we are all creatures made in
God's image, what must we each work toward becoming? *(a peacemaker)* Divide the
class into pairs or small groups. Ask each group to list five qualities they think a
peacemaker should have. *(Possible answers: patience, kindness, ability to compromise,*
calm, hopefulness). After they have completed the activity, invite each group to share
its list with the class. Ask students why the qualities they listed are important for a
peacemaker. Ask them to consider how many of the qualities they have and which
qualities they would like to develop.

Peace Is Always in Our Prayers *(page 120)*

Bring prayer books to class and show your students examples of prayers in which the
word *shalom* appears. Examples are Shalom Rav *(Siddur Sim Shalom, 1998, page 44;*
Gates of Prayer, 1975, page 46; Kol Haneshamah, 1994, page 105) and Hashkiveinu
(Siddur Sim Shalom, 1998, page 33; Gates of Prayer, 1975, page 133; Kol Haneshamah,
1994, page 81). You also may invite your students to locate other examples of
prayers that speak of peace.

 Artist's Corner: Peace Is Always in Our Prayers *(page 120)*

Prepare a piece of butcher-block paper at least ten to fifteen feet long and drawing
supplies, such as crayons, markers, and colored pencils. In addition, have handy a
camera and film. (A disposable camera will do.) Explain to students that in the
Hashkiveinu prayer (see above activity for location in prayer book) we ask God to
spread over us "Your shelter of peace," *sukkat sh'lomecha.* Ask students what other
Hebrew word sounds like *sukkat. (Sukkot)* Ask what the name of the shelter we build
in honor of the holiday of Sukkot is. *(a sukkah)* Tell students they will now construct
a Sukkah of Peace.

Lay the butcher-block paper on the floor and invite students to decorate it with
scenes of peace, quotes about peace from the prayer book, and their own good wishes
for peace. Then ask students what can be used to hold up the Sukkah of Peace
besides poles, walls, or other materials? *(The students can.)* Invite the students to
support the sukkah by standing under it and holding it up with their hands. Point
out to students that the best way to ensure that they live under a shelter of peace is
to work with others to create and support peace.

Take photographs of the students under the sukkah as a souvenir and reminder
of the experience. You may also want to photograph the pictures and sayings with
which the students decorated the sukkah. Consider submitting pictures to your
synagogue news bulletin or website.

There's No Place Like Home *(pages 121–123)*

Tell students that the ancient sage Rabbi Shimon ben Yoḥai taught, "The most difficult of all mitzvot is: Honor your parents" *(Tanḥuma, Ekev 2).* Ask students why they
think this might be so. *(Possible answers: It's hard to follow all the rules parents require.*

Parents are sometimes unfair to kids. You're with your parents a lot and you can't always be good.)

Ask students how they might apply the teaching of Rabbi Tarfon (introduced on page 44 of the textbook) to honoring their parents: "It is not your duty to complete the work; neither are you free to stop persisting" (*Pirkei Avot* 2:16). *(Possible answers: Persist in making improvements to my behavior. When I'm upset, take a deep breath before speaking. Instead of acting out, let my dad know what I am feeling. Remember to tell my mom that I love and appreciate her.)*

Photo Op *(page 122)*

Invite students to describe what they do with their families that gives them a feeling of peace.

It Happens in Every Family *(page 123)*

Have students read and work through this activity individually. Keep in mind that many students live in homes where there are stresses and conflicts that are outside their control. Therefore, it is important to acknowledge that while each person can contribute to making a home *more* peaceful, no one person can make a home *completely* peaceful. Do not press students who prefer not to share their responses to do so.

Pursue Peace in the Jewish Community *(page 124)*

Ask: Why is God called the "Maker "and not the "Giver" of Peace? *(Peace is not something that can be given; peace is achieved through two or more parties working to create an agreement. God works through human beings to make peace.)*

Bible Bio and Extraordinary Acts *(page 126)*

After students have read both features, ask: What is the connection between Isaiah's words and Rabin's hope for a "farewell to arms"? *(Both men tried to inspire others to work toward a peaceful world, a world without weapons.)*

Ask students what they can do to help make Isaiah's words come true and to honor the memory of Yitzḥak Rabin. *(Contribute tzedakah to organizations that promote peace; volunteer at organizations that help feed and shelter the needy; boycott movies and video games that treat violence as entertainment.)*

Point out that the tragedy of Rabin's assassination was that much greater because he was murdered by another Jew. Not only did Yigal Amir commit the crime of murder, he also did not honor the tradition of *klal Yisra'el* (the unity of the Jewish people).

Teaching Enrichment: Ancient Stories for Modern Times

(page 127)

Invite students to discuss whether or not they think the Muslim poet should have been punished for lying about the poem. *(Yes: With no consequence for lying, he will be*

more likely to lie again. No: It was better to show him compassion and make a friend of him, which will make him less likely to lie in the future.)

Ask students what they think motivated Ibn Nagrela to respond as he did to the Muslim poet. *(Possible answers: strength of character—it would have been easier to respond with violence as the king suggested; his good impulse, or* yetzer hatov; *his knowledge of Jewish values)*

Learn It & Live It *(page 129)*

Possible answer for question 2, part 1: We usually get along with our friends, and our disagreements with them are relatively minor. It is with our enemies that we have the greatest difficulty and need for making peace. We often have very different—even opposing—points of view and interests from our enemies, which adds to the difficulty.

Possible answer for question 2, part 2: I try to improve my relationship with people with whom I have difficulty getting along. I can try to be open-minded rather than rigid or offensive when I deal with people I don't care for.

 ## Family in Action

Encourage students to share with their families the strategies and techniques they have learned for adding peace at home—*sh'lom bayit*. Ask families to brainstorm additional strategies and techniques, and to try to implement them on Shabbat. Invite students to share the lists their families brainstormed and to tell about their successes and failures in implementing these ideas, as well as their plans for working toward improvement.

THE VALUE OF PEACE

CHAPTER 11

THE Matter OF Balance

Textbook pages 130–139

Core Concept

Our tradition teaches us to strive to live balanced lives—caring for ourselves and treating others with respect, studying to increase our knowledge, and taking action to help improve the world.

Learning Objectives

Students will be able to:

❋ Discuss biblical role models who balanced self-interest with commitment to others.

❋ Describe three actions they can take that have built-in balance.

❋ List three ways in which they can continue to transform their growing Jewish knowledge into actions that help improve the world.

Chapter Overview

This chapter teaches the importance of balancing self-interest with concern for others. It encourages students to think in terms of growth and improvement rather than perfection, and to turn their ever-expanding wisdom into actions that help improve the world.

 ## Getting Started: Unpacking the Text

(pages 130–131)

Invite a student to read aloud *Pirkei Avot* 1:14 on page 130. Ask students to describe the type of people Hillel is encouraging us to be. *(people who balance their needs with those of society, who are self-reliant but not selfish, and who don't procrastinate)* Ask: Why does our tradition teach that we each must be for ourselves? *(All people are made in God's image, so our first duty is to treat ourselves with respect.)*

Ask students to describe actions they take that show they are for themselves. *(eat healthily, study, exercise, play video games)* What actions show they are not only for themselves? *(give up a seat on the bus for an older person, help clear dinner dishes from the table, contribute tzedakah)*

Invite three volunteers to each read aloud a portion of the story on page 131. Ask students which character observed Hillel's teaching. *(the woman, who took care of herself by speaking respectfully to the king, who helped her community by speaking up, and tried to teach the king a lesson about how to treat his people)*

Tell students that in this chapter they will learn about the importance of balancing concern for themselves with concern for others.

Our Tradition Guides Us *(pages 132–135)*

Bring in a balance scale, a picture of one, or draw one on the chalkboard or a large piece of butcher-block paper. (If you do a search for "balance scale" on www.google.com you will find pictures of a variety of balance scales.) Ask your students to think of an action they can take that symbolizes being for themselves *(buying a CD they want)* and an action that symbolizes being for others. *(volunteering to help clean up after a Purim carnival or party)*

If you have a balance scale, hand each student two marbles (or some other small objects that can be weighed). One at a time, invite students to come up to the scale. Students should put a marble on the right side of the scale to symbolize actions taken for themselves. On the left side, students should place a marble representative of actions taken for others. (If you have a picture of a balance scale, students can write their actions on small self-adhesive papers and place them on either side of the picture. If you draw a picture of the scale, students can write their responses directly on the chalkboard or butcher-block paper.)

Engage students in a discussion of what their lives might be like if their actions were limited to those only on the right-hand side of the scale. What if they were limited to those only on the left side? Ask: How can balancing concern for yourself with concern for others improve the quality of your life? (*Possible answers: It can help me take care of myself, increase my ability to make friends, encourage others help me when I need assistance, make me feel useful.*)

Ancient Stories for Modern Times (page 133)

Invite two students to each read aloud a portion of the story. Have the class complete the activity and share their answers. (*Recording our heroes' mistakes as well as their achievements reminds us that no one is perfect; if our heroes can make mistakes and still be role models, then we, too, can be worthy despite our mistakes.*)

Bible Bio (page 134)

You may want to invite your cantor or music specialist to teach students the song "Eiliyahu Hanavi" ("Elijah the Prophet"), which we sing at the end of Shabbat, after the *havdalah* ceremony, and at the Passover seder.

 Photo Op (pages 134–135)

Ask students how remembering the story of Rabbi Akiva on page 133 can help them when they've made a mistake and feel badly.

The Extraordinary Acts of Ordinary People (page 136)

Invite volunteers to read aloud the text. Explain that, like Tovah Lieberman, everyone who is described in the book's "The Extraordinary Acts of Ordinary People" features began to help make the world a better place when they were young. In fact, many started when they were around the same age as the students, by helping their family, friends, and neighbors. Over time, the skills and independence of Tovah and the others grew and they were not only able to help themselves and the people who were closest to them, but also to reach out to the larger world.

Explain that helping others sometimes only requires that we share our interests and talents. Ask students what they can do to benefit others. (*use their love of pets to walk an elderly neighbor's dog, share their sense of humor or ability to sing or play a musical instrument with residents of a nursing home, use their knitting skills to knit scarves or hats for homeless children, use their knowledge of math or Hebrew to tutor younger children*)

Artist's Corner: The Messiah Is Ready When We Are

(pages 138–139)

Read aloud the story on pages 138–139. Ask students what types of actions they can take to help bring the Messiah closer. *(perform mitzvot, give tzedakah, take good care of their own health, speak respectfully to others, balance justice with mercy)*

Invite the class to create a mural portraying a path filled with the actions they can take to help bring the Messiah closer. Have the path lead to a scene of what they think the world will look like in the days after the Messiah's coming. (You may want to discuss the illustration on page 139 before your students begin their work.) You can use butcher-block paper and art supplies such as crayons, markers, magazine pictures, and glue. The mural may make a good decoration for a school hallway. You may want to photograph it for your synagogue's website.

Accommodations FOR Students WITH Special Needs

Children vary in their learning styles. Some students learn best with a hands-on approach, while others do best with a visual or an auditory approach. In general, teachers who present material in many different ways will be able to reach many more children.

Teachers of children with special needs have additional challenges. These children include those with a broad range of cognitive, physical, and behavioral disabilities that have an impact on learning. It is always helpful to find out from parents what accommodations are made for their child in secular school. The suggestions included below are primarily for those children with learning, perceptual, or attention problems.

For the student with attention and auditory processing problems: Teach in small increments and, when presenting directions, present one direction at a time. Ask the child to repeat the direction to be sure he or she has processed it.

For the child with attention problems: Limit teaching segments to 10–15 minutes, and allow for movement between activities.

For the child with decoding problems: Make flashcards with a few key words. The child can take them home and practice them with his or her parents. Keep a shoebox of flashcards for children who need them.

For the child with attention and visual figure-ground problems: Mask parts of the page so the child can see only the section that is being worked on.

For the child with fine-motor and handwriting problems: Limit the amount of writing, drawing, and cutting that is required. The teacher may do such difficult parts of a project and allow the student to finish the task. Or, precut or trace in advance the complex elements if appropriate.

Other suggestions that can benefit all children include:

❊ Provide opportunities for choral reading rather than asking children to read aloud individually.

❊ Use concrete objects whenever possible so that students can learn, or reinforce their learning, through their senses. For example, on page 101 of *Count Me In*, when teaching the prayer for fragrant plants, you might bring in a bouquet of flowers for the students to touch and smell.

✳ Use a highlighter to visibly showcase an activity or information.

✳ Encourage students to work independently or cooperatively, whichever brings them a better sense of comfort and confidence.

✳ When students work collaboratively, make sure all students are participating in the group. If possible, assign each group member a specific role (for example, recorder, reader, presenter).

✳ Permit students time to finish an activity or reduce the number of items or steps in the activity.